T0195987

During a Pandemic

Written by ASHLEY PERROTTI

Illustrated by FAZAL NABBIE

Archway Publishing books may be ordered through booksellers or by contacting:

Archway Publishing
1663 Liberty Drive
Bloomington, IN 47403
www.archwaypublishing.com
844-669-3957

ISBN: 978-1-6657-0391-8 (sc)
ISBN: 978-1-6657-0459-5 (hc)
ISBN: 978-1-6657-0390-1 (e)

Print information available on the last page.

Archway Publishing rev. date: 03/23/2021

Dedication

To my daughters Grace and Abigail,

I will never forget the year we were home.
Time that felt stolen from us, but in the
end we see that it was time given.

I promise to always give you the world, even
when it feels like the world is falling apart.

I love you.

There is something called a pandemic,
it's when a virus spreads around.

Those who catch this virus get sneezes,
coughs, and frowns.

During a pandemic the schools and churches close.

Not for long, just for a bit, so don't wash your fancy clothes!

During a pandemic we watch important people on TV.

Mom and Dad call it 'the news' and they listen, watch, and see.

During a pandemic there are essential things we need every day.

We need doctors, groceries, and mail that's on its way.

During a pandemic we spend more time at home.

We spend extra time with family and we think
of those who are alone.

During a pandemic we wash hands more than ever before.

We cover when we sneeze, keep hands to ourselves, and take shoes off at the door.

During a pandemic we miss our grandmas, cousins, and friends too.

Remember this I beg you, you're lucky to have people to miss, and who miss you.

AFTER a pandemic people jump with glee!

Schools to open, parties to plan, and movies for all to see!

After a pandemic we may still wear masks, you see.

You'll get used to them I promise, and safer you will be.

After a pandemic you know what important means to you.

Things that are important, like who you love
and who loves you.

Printed in the United States
by Baker & Taylor Publisher Services